The
One Minute Book Marketer

25 Quick Ways to Sell More Books Today

Brought to you by
Author's Success Guild

Dr. Bette Daoust
Wendy Dewar Hughes

Author's
Success Guild

For Your Free Report on How to Get
Media Attention

http://bookmarketing.authorssuccessguild.com/getmedia

Copyright 2015 © Author's Success Guild

Dr. Bette Daoust and Wendy Dewar Hughes

Website: www.authorssuccessguild.com

Editing, Interior Design and Cover Design: Wendy Dewar Hughes, Summer Bay Press

ISBN: 978-0-9947353-0-0
Digital ISBN: 978-0-9947353-1-7

TABLE OF CONTENTS

Networking for Your Target Audience

I know who the target audience is for my books but I'm having trouble connecting with them. How do I network with my readers?

Networking is a very loosely used term. It can encompass many forms such as face-to-face meetings, group meetings, virtual presentations, social media discussions, and informal gatherings.

The bigger issue is that you need to define your perfect readers before deciding how to network with them.

If you know they always go to library talks, attend webinars given by authors, or hang out on Pinterest, then you have the basis for building a relationship with your readers.

Here are five tactics you can use to connect with your readers.

1. Be interested in them. Do not talk about yourself, take the time to learn as much as you can when it comes to interests, wants, and needs. All of these

bits of information will help you to better target your approach to gaining your own following.

2. Talk in terms of reader benefits. Readers are only interested in themselves and by concentrating on what is in it for them (WIIFT) you will have a better chance of grabbing their attention.

3. Be a part of the conversation. Add your comments without the sales approach, be the one that shares readily. Readers will be sure to find out more about you when you offer free advice and share on a regular basis.

4. Be an advocate for the reader. Find reasons to support their reading needs. Offer suggestions and even offer parts of your own work.

5. Direct them to some of your social media platforms by asking for input. Ask and you shall get followers and potential readers for your books.

With these tactics in hand, you will still need to constantly feed information and follow up, and through, with conversations. Being there consistently shows you are truly interested in them. Show up sporadically and you will likely be dismissed as someone who is just trying to sell his or her wares.

So how can you be consistent with keeping up on all the conversations?

Start your day with a list of places to visit and make comments. Add time snippets to your day to add to conversations. At Author's Success Guild, we add to some of our social media platforms first thing in the morning, check the status a couple of times during the day to make sure there is nothing urgent to answer and finally look at our statistics for our entries at the end of the day.

We use a number of tools to help us with the process. We use Tweetdeck for our twitter feeds, Hootsuite to do scheduling of posts and monitor responses, and direct messaging for our groups. Being informed about what is happening at all times keeps us busy and it keeps us involved and responding to reader needs. You should consider doing the same.

What's in a Plan Anyway?

I feel like I need some kind of plan to move my writing career forward but I hardly know where to begin. What would a marketing plan for a serious author look like anyway?

Can you get 3000 likes without advertising? Can you do it within 4 weeks?

The answer should be a resounding YES!

Now you may be thinking, right, like I can do that without advertising the heck out of my fan page. The truth is that anyone can do it as long as you have the right tools in place.

1. Set a goal. According to Yogi Berra, "If you don't know where you are going, you'll end up someplace else." Nothing is further from the truth when it comes to setting a goal for your social media networks. Our goal at Author's Success Guild was to have 5000 followers in the first year. Although that sounds small and big at the same time, we also included a goal of not using advertising as we wanted only people that

are not just responding to an ad but only those that really wanted to be a part of our page. Less than a year later, we are almost there, only a few more weeks and our goal will be accomplished.

2. Plan content a year in advance. This does not mean you have write or produce the content, it simply means that you want to have everything planned out before you write a word. Use a spreadsheet or tools such as OneNote to create a planning grid. We use theme-based content to organize our work. Once the themes and topics for each theme are in place (we do twelve themes for a year with a minimum of twelve topics for each theme), you can then review your plan and make changes quite easily.

3. Plan your action items for your content. What calls to action do you want to use and when? Add a column to your spreadsheet and add these to your plan. If your call to action could be as simple as LIKE my page. You can add others such as Join our Mailing List, or Enter a Contest. The choice is yours. By adding items to your plan, you will be sure to complete the task.

4. Plan your hashtags and keywords. Research the keywords you will be using to attract readers. Do it through using the right hashtags and writing content that uses a maximum of three keywords. Know what these are ahead of producing any

content. The more you know about your perfect reader, the easier it is to attract them to your page.

5. Follow your plan! Although we have not added a lot of the budgeting, operations, or other normal things to the plan, we have a plan for our content to achieve a defined goal. Now is the time to follow that plan.

6. Write content that is shareable. Your content needs to spark emotions that inspire the reader to say, "Wow, I have to share this with my followers, and friends."

7. Finally, start by writing at least two months of content to begin the process.

It all Starts with a Font

For branding, does it matter if I use different font faces for all my materials?

From experience, I know that reading something that has many different fonts, styles, and colors will certainly attract attention, yet it does not show professionalism. When I see those kinds of materials, I often think that it must be a homemade, hobby-driven organization rather than a place I would go to get an expert opinion.

Although some experts, the true experts, will often just post plain text in a boxy looking website, I still know that they are the expert and just not too tech savvy.

My preference is to have a more professional and polished look and feel. You can still use graphics that use alternates for fonts but generally you want to use one that works well with your logo and brand. Our logo for Author's Success Guild as shown above is a good example of using a font that fits with the image. It is simple serif font that is clear and easy to read.

When you see our logo, you know, in general terms, we are a guild that helps authors be successful.

Here are some tips to help you choose the right font for your branding effort:

1. Choose a font that is easy to read. Nothing is worse than squinting to read a scripted or cute font on a business card. People want to know what you do and they want to recognize a well-designed card, brochure, poster, logo, and more. Make it easy for them to read your materials.

2. Choose one font for headlines and a complementary one for the body of your text. Headlines are often san-serif while body text has serifs. A font like Univers works for titles in your book while Bookman is more suitable for your body text. Each font works for the application selected. Reverse them and it is not so pleasing to the eye.

3. Choose a good font size for each application. Titles and headlines are normally larger in size and often up to 72 pts., while body text tends to be 10 to 12 pts. in size. Although larger font sizes attract attention, it does not mean that large volumes of text are easy to digest in that format.

4. Look at your paragraph and line spacing. When you have chosen your fonts, look at them when used in paragraphs and blocks of text. Does the

spacing work for your font? Some fonts look better with tight or single line spacing while others look better at 1.15 or 1.5 lines of spacing. Use what works for your materials.

5. Web fonts are different than print fonts. You will not always be able to use the font of your choosing when it comes the materials being displayed on web pages, blogs, or other locations. Not all browsers support many of the fonts provided for print media. Do your best by also choosing web fonts for your work. In reality, you may not have much of a choice when posting materials but you can control some of it on your own website.

Creating Presentation Assets, Five Tips to Success

I love presentations but each one is different. Should I be keeping all my assets such as images and links consistent for every presentation I do?

People are always asking me questions around what to do for presentations, especially when it comes to branding. There are two camps here.

1. In order to have something new and fresh each time out, a different template can be used as long as the logo and website links remain constant. While this is great for many speakers, depending on their topic, it is not so great when it comes to establishing your brand.

2. Keep the same template with logo and website link but vary the slide layouts. This style gives you a lot of flexibility and still has you maintain recognizable brand standards. If you have two different series of books, you can use one template and switch up the color schemes and fonts. There will be no loss in brand recognition

of you the author, and each book series will have a color and font style.

Now let's talk further about presentations assets.

The only images that should not change are your logo and perhaps the professional photo you are using. Although you may change the professional photo, it is unlikely you will change your logo for a long period of time.

1. Here are five tips that will give you an edge when it

2. If the image is a logo then the name of the file should be LOGO-logoname-logoSize. For example LOGO-ASG10x103 or LOGO-ASG-Large500x350. As you can see all the logo files will be listed together. You can do the same for your other images and use key terms such as AuthorPhoto, BookCover, and so on.

   a. Using the image size in the file name aids in knowing which file you want to use when preparing your next presentation.

3. Keep track of all the links you use in presentations. Use OneNote, EverNote, or other filing system to keep a list of the links and where you have used them. This will do two things for you.

a. You do not have to rummage through presentations to find the links you want to reference.

b. It gives you the ability to test the links from time to time and, if need be, you can update the references to the link.

4. One last item to keep on hand—action items. Make a list of the action items you want to use in a presentation and the links and webpages or landing pages that are the target. Keeping such a list handy makes it easier than trying to remember what you did last time.

Keep track of everything you use. File the assets on a regular basis.

Gossip is Cheap, Why Not Use It To Your Advantage?

We all know that gossip is a dirty word but how do I get people to start talking about me, and my book, so I don't look sleazy?

The definition of gossip is usually unconstrained, out of context, derogatory conversation about other people. It could be betraying a confidence, making hurtful judgements, or even spreading information that is sensitive and can cause pain.

So why do people spread gossip?

1. They want attention on themselves. They want to be the place where others get the inside scoop.

2. They are envious of the other person and want to find ways to bring them down to their own level. It is like the crabs in a pot. When one almost gets out, the others pull it down. Gossip is no different.

3. They want group consensus. The feeling of belonging to a group by bringing others down is not uncommon.

4. They are unhappy in their current situation and by gossiping they feel a sense of righteousness by making disparaging remarks.

5. They want to rouse interest from others to gain attention. They want to feel better about themselves, so make hurtful negative judgement on others.

Now you know the reasons why people gossip, how can you tap into the ongoing gossip to your own advantage without becoming a nasty gossip yourself? I am not sure if the people doing the gossiping are the people you really want to have on your mailing list, but who knows where they will spread the word?

1. Give them something to gossip about, such as an insider secret that they are not supposed to share with anyone. Knowing ahead of time that the secret will be shared immediately, make sure the secret is something that will benefit your book sales.

2. Boast about an award and let them talk about how you should not have received it. Be sure you feed them the page where the award is displayed. I am sure that this will be shared as well, along

with the negative comments. Your response here is, "Well, read it for yourself to see if that is true."

3.   Always give a gossiper fuel that benefits you. Go back to your reader benefits and create juicy tidbits a gossiper would love to share behind your back. It is like saying, "This is a secret; don't tell anyone!"

Gossip can be directed in your favor. You have to make sure you are feeding the right information and guiding people to the right place to add their comments. Sometimes negative comments can be turned around with great responses. Do not defend yourself, just present the facts.

The results? More readers and gossipers on your side.

What's Trending and What's Not?

Social media seems to change so fast, and everyone says you have to be on all these different media? It's all so overwhelming. How can I know what's the best place for me to spend my social media time and energy?

The best answer to this question is, "What is important to you?"

Where are you getting the most brand recognition?

Where are most of your readers hanging out?

Where are the bulk of your sales coming from?

If you can answer these questions, then at least you will have an idea around how many of the social media networks you need to monitor.

Here are several places you can use to monitor your social media networks.

1. Tweetdeck.com. Here you can add all your twitter profiles and watch your mentions, retweets, and more. You can also get a handle on what is trending and the number of follows you are getting on a daily basis.

2. HootSuite. Although you can only use three profiles in the free version, Hootsuite certainly allows you to monitor many streams of information.

   a. You can manage trend searches by adding a stream for each search. I use this to find new sites for my research when I am writing a new book.

   b. You can add RSS feeds through an app called Syndicate App. If you have sites you are monitoring for new ideas, trends in the market place or just to keep an eye on the competition, then this is a great place to start.

3. Other tools. There are literally hundreds of other management tools available for keeping track of all your social media networks. Obviously there are far too many to list here. The two we have mentioned in this article are the two top places to start. The point here is that you do start monitoring your activities and scheduling your input.

Now let's take a look at what Google has to offer you when it comes to trends. Google has a product called Google Trends https://www.google.com/trends/ and here is how it works:

There are three initial areas on the intro screen as seen here. By the way, you can change countries at the top to get the trends for other areas.

There are hundreds of thousands of newsletters out there and each has a niche and genre they serve. A newsletter is a fantastic way to keep in touch with your readers on a regular basis. Your newsletter should be more than what you blog or share on social media. It needs to go above and beyond to keep your audience interested.

Yes friends, family, and others close to you will be the first line of attack. Why not use them as a place to get criticism and feedback. Use this information to improve your newsletter and get it ready for your readers. There's nothing better than using what will happen anyway to your advantage.

Think of your newsletter as another product you are releasing.

Now let's think about how you will be sharing your newsletter, even before you have a list of readers in place. Here are some ideas you can use for your distribution.

1. Email the newsletter in its entirety as an attachment. This certainly works, however, it does not guarantee that the recipient will open the newsletter. Also, the file may be large and slow down some readers computers.

2. Send an email with highlights from the newsletter with links to the full articles. I receive many of these each day. This way I can scan the headlines and decide if there is anything I want to read.

3. Send an email with just a link to the latest edition. This is one where you have no idea what is in the newsletter and its takes a decision and some effort on my part to click and then read it.

4. Mail a printed copy to your list. Hmmm....this one is very expensive. Some larger organizations do this but most newsletters today are in E-format.

5. Produce a news magazine and publish it through a magazine site similar to the e-versions of many popular magazines.

Our preference is the highlighted version #2. The reader then can hold on to your email for a later scan or click directly on the link to get the info they want.

Now it is time to decide where to get readers for your newsletter. Gaining readers is not an easy task and you do have to work on it over a long period of time. Here are some ideas you can implement immediately.

1. Tweet about your newsletter - include a link for a sample newsletter on a landing page that captures email addresses to be added to your list.

2. Post the same information on Facebook and LinkedIn.

3. Post a graphic that advertises your newsletter on Pinterest.

4. List your newsletter in newsletter directories.

5. Advertise for readers on Facebook, Twitter, or LinkedIn.

Now you are armed with some ways to increase your reader base. Good luck with your newsletter. Send us a link so we can read it, too!

Repurposing Your Content—How to Write Once and Distribute Many Times

I have written some articles and posted on article sites but writing these takes time. Are there ways that I can re-use the same content in different ways to extend my reach without re-inventing the wheel?

Writing does take time and often time is really limited, especially when you are writing your next book, spending time marketing your current publication, and trying to juggle research and family life. Whew, even the thought of it makes me tired. Do you ever feel that marketing is so time consuming that you cannot possibly do a great job doing all that is required?

Congratulations on the fact that you have written some articles. Now let's take these articles and start re-using the content to create even more marketing collateral.

Here are some creative ways to extend the life of your writing. Use all of them or use only a few—the choice is yours. Implementing just one or two of these ideas will save you time.

1. Create a graphic by using a quote from your article. You can actually create several graphics. The graphic should include a website URL and your logo. You want to make sure the graphic brands you and that it drives viewers to your landing page. You will now have images to post on Pinterest and other social media networks.

2. Create a podcast series from your articles. Get someone to introduce you and your topic then read your article. The final part of the podcast should include a summary and a call to action for the listeners. Do this for each of your articles.

3. Create a mini YouTube show. Prepare slide decks based on your article and do a voice over then save the presentations as an mp4 and post it to YouTube, Vimeo, or other video site. When posting videos, write a description and video summary that includes a call to action.

4. Create a presentation based on your article. Add animations and transitions. Your presentation should be able to stand on its own. Post the presentation to SlideShare and other slide sharing sites. Oh, yes, don't forget to include contact, website, and a call to action in the slide deck.

5. Create a mini book of your articles and publish it to Kindle's KDP program. Add a table of contents and summary. Include a call to action in the book. This is a great place to drive people to your other books.

6. Expand your articles so they are very detailed and unique. Post an offering on Fiverr or similar site and sell your articles. One note here. Your article needs to be unique and exclusive to Fiverr. You will also need to create an offering trailer to be posted on their site.

7. Create a set of questions around your article. Pose these questions on sites such as LinkedIn or in Forums. Remember that your profile in these locations is the primary way people can contact you.

8. Create a course using your articles as the basis of disseminating your information. Courses are not that difficult to create and you can easily grow your audience through sites such as Udemy or Fedora.

9. Syndicate your article series. Offer them to newspapers or magazines.

10. Add your articles to newsletters, particularly your own. Adjust the content to make it different but the same topic.

More work? For sure! The effort is definitely worth it as your reader base will start to grow from many different angles.

Simple Audio Recording Tricks for Creating a Podcast

I have been thinking of recording a series of podcasts but I'm not sure what software or programs to use that I don't have to spend a lot of time learning. Can anyone suggest simple ways for me to get started with podcasting?

Podcasting is a great tool for marketing your books. If you already have some recordings, then perhaps it is time to create a podcast series.

Podcasting is not just having one or two audios ready to go, podcasting is a commitment to producing a program on a regular basis. Your readers will expect to hear your podcasts based on a schedule. Think about the commitment you want to make before posting your recordings.

Here are some suggestions for getting started on your podcasting journey.

1. Set up an account with iTunes and post your recordings as part of a series. iTunes lists hundreds of podcast channels and is a great place

to start. You will still have to do your own promotion and drive people to the link.

2. SoundCloud offers space to host your podcasts. They offer free and paid plans. Although the free version does have its limitations, it is a great place to start.

3. Archive.org Is one of the most well-known places for hosting a podcast. They allow you to upload a large variety of media files including mp3s. They also offer many embedding options.

4. Amazon S3. This location requires a payment. They offer a high quality hosting service and the price is lower than most other paid hosting services. Just a note here - as your subscriber base increases, so will your hosting fees.

5. OurMedia.org. This hosting service is completely free. There are no limits on bandwidth, and the uploads are quite fast. They do scan your content to make sure it fits within their defined boundaries.

6. Podomatic is also a free podcast host service. Your account has 15 GB of bandwidth each month and around 500 GB of storage. The best part, you can also create your podcasts directly on the site.

7. Libsyn is one of the longest running podcast site around. They host thousands of shows with over

a billion downloads. The service is not free with the lowest plan being $5 per month and 50 GB of storage.

8. Podbean is another easy-to-use podcast hosting site. This one also has a free option with under 30 GB of storage.

9. Buzzsprout offers both free and paid subscriptions. This site also allows files that are 2 hours long! You can store your podcasts here indefinitely with a cost starting at $12 per month.

10. Your own site. You can load your podcasts to your own website and have people register to listen to your work. This takes more time and effort and depends on how much you want to put into it.

Creating Media Kits That Shout

What is a Media Kit? I heard that it is just a press release and a copy of your book.

You have probably heard the term Press Kit as well as Media Kit. The reality is that these are both the same. The Media kit is an information package about your book and you as the author.

Many media kits are different for each usage. You will have a kit for the press and you will also have a kit for book reviewers. Most often authors make the mistake of using the same kit for both locations. Not all the information you provide will be relevant for reviewers and the same is true for the media.

Let's talk about what goes into a media kit and then we will talk about the differences for each application. This first list is what you should have ready when looking for interviews. Before you send all the information out, spend time making sure your genre is ideal for the media you have selected. Media often wants to be pitched first and then upon acceptance, the media kit is sent.

28

1. A letter of introduction.

2. Information on you as the author.

3. Summary information about your book.

4. Recent press coverage and articles.

5. Any press releases you have issued.

6. Audio and video files of interviews, speeches, and other media events.

7. A sample news story that you would like to see in print.

8. News relating to genre trends.

9. A list of at least ten questions you could be asked when being interviewed.

10. A list of awards and contest placements.

11. Author professional photo.

12. Book Cover graphics.

13. Promotion events that you have scheduled.

14. Camera-ready logo art if you have a series or brand you are promoting.

15. An order form.

16. Resource sheet that includes links to your website and social media networks.

17. Contact Information.

Sometimes you can include the full copy of your book. If you are physically mailing your materials, this can be expensive. To reduce costs, spend time building relationships with the media and reviewers ahead of sending out the kit.

The Media Kit for Reviewers

Reviewers are only interested in knowing you have a great book to present to the public. However, they do like to know a little about you and your work before doing the review. I know you can get reviewers by just sending out your book, but you are not really getting the most out of your efforts by not sending the media kit.

Send the reviewers the following:

1. The letter of introduction.

2. Information on you as the author.

3. Summary information about your book.

4. Press coverage you have already received.

5. List of awards.

6. An e-copy of your book. (PDF is preferable as it can be read easily on most computer screens.)

7. Contact information and website link.

Reviewers do not likely need any other information but if they are truly interested, they will get back to you and ask for more.

Although there is a lot of material in a media kit, having it all ready to go ahead of any media coverage or book review will save you a great deal of time and effort.

Paid or Free—What works better When it Comes to Advertising?

What can advertising do for me? Is it not just as easy to build my list without it?

Let's look at both methods of advertising. First, free advertising is a misnomer as it takes time to grow your list using organic methods. You will have to build relationships with potential readers one at a time. You may not spend a lot of money but it will cost you time.

Using good search engine optimization is one piece of the puzzle. It allows you to closely match the users' queries. If your reader is looking for thriller books and they type in "new thriller books", you want your information to be on the top of the list.

Be an active participant in groups. Join groups on the various social media networks and then contribute. You will soon gather a following and be able to add those individuals to your list. With groups, ACTIVE participation is the key to fame. Be active in only a few groups at a time, as you do not want to be spending all day just answering questions or offering your expert advice. When your follower numbers get large enough (over 1,000) then it is time to create your own group. Populate the group with your current followers from each of the groups where you participate. You will still need to be active in the other groups as that is the feed mechanism for your current group.

If you are using Twitter, follow people in your genre or people reading the genre. Choose carefully who you follow as you want to follow those with larger lists. Quite often they will follow you back. That is exactly what you want. If they do not follow you back, find ways to retweet much of their material to capture some of their followers. Although this does not work all the time, it will help to build your list.

Use Pinterest to build a following as well. This will take some effort, as you need to post images. You can repost images you find on other pages, which will help boost, your followers. You should also be creating your own images, as the uniqueness will often get shared, which in turn builds your list.

Post shareables to Facebook with your branding in place. Be consistent with your postings.

Build a presentation and place it on SlideShare. SlideShare provides an easy way to add recognition and build your list.

There are many more ways to build your list organically and all of them take some work.

As for paid advertising, this can give you faster growth in a shorter period of time. By composing the right ad, with the right keywords, and the right image, your list of followers can hit over 1,000 within a few weeks. At Vital Health Review, the list of Facebook followers increased from a meagre 15 to 1400 in three weeks. That list has not declined in over eight months.

The biggest decision is which direction to take. At Author's Success Guild we take a hybrid approach. We build organically in the initial stages and also build content at the same time. When we reach a pre-determined threshold we then buy advertising space. With building first we know that there is a market for our offerings and then the paid advertising is not a waste of money.

Secrets of Book Sales by Using Character Chronicles

I understand Kindle, and other locations too, like you to have several books published before they promote your book.

It seems like having more than one book in the mix is the trend these days. We are told that no one wants to just read a one book wonder author. I often disagree with this statement as some of the greatest work is all in one volume. Having said that, you really will get more attention if you have a series of books to sell.

How can you do this without writing another huge volume of material?

If you are like most authors, you have probably done a lot of research when it comes to your characters, location, and the period costumes. You have likely though about your characters and their back-story. All of this is fodder for a mini book.

Here are some ideas to get more books out before the second book of your series.

1. Readers get involved with your characters. They want to know more about them and their flaws.

2. Think about your characters traits. What mini story can you put together about them before they entered your book world.

3. Write about the costume designs and the latest trends for the period of your story. Perhaps add material around how to make the costumes.

4. Write about the perils of travel.

5. Write a cookbook using recipes of the time.

Although there are many more ways you can add mini books, these are a good start.

Now for non-fiction writers, it could be a little simpler.

Here are some ideas for non-fiction writers:

1. Take your original works and divide it into chapters then add a great deal of detail around each chapter to form a mini-book. For example, an eleven-chapter book could be broken up into eleven mini-books.

2. Create instructional guides for your book.

3. Create workbooks. There are some incredible workbooks for trending books.

4. Take all your blog articles together to make another book. I know of a few people who have done this very successfully.

5. Write materials around client discussions and stated problems.

6. Start a group and ask questions. Use the answers as the basis of a new mini-book.

No matter what you decide to do, publishing more than one or two books will certainly give you a head start when it comes to being recognized as the authority on your subject matter.

Displaying at Trade Shows

I have been invited to be part of a local consumer trade show. I don't want to just sit behind a table and hope someone looks in my direction. Can you give me tips or ideas on how to make my booth irresistible?

Every serious writer knows that attending writers' conferences is valuable on many levels. Workshops help you develop your craft, with topics covering everything from character arcs to antique firearms. You will meet many other authors and get to hang out with people who understand how your mind works, because theirs works the same way.

Many writers' conferences also include visits from editors and literary agents seeking to meet authors and hopefully discover the next publishing sensation, or at least contract for some well-written books that will help everyone stay in business.

One of the features that may or may not be held at a writers' conference is a book fair. A book fair is an opportunity for attending authors and publishers to set up a booth or table showcasing their books for the other attendees of the event or the buying public.

If the book fair is open to the public, that's even better. You want to be able to expose your books to as many new pairs of eyes as possible. While it's great to be able to sell your books to your peers – writers are usually also prolific readers – what you want is to find new readers from the book-buying public.

So how do you go about getting into a book fair as a selling author? First of all, when considering a writers' conference to attend, be sure to search the conference website and find out if the event will include a book fair and if it will be open and advertised to the public. This may influence which conference you decide to attend. If all other things are more or less equal, why not attend the event where you have the opportunity to make some sales and find new fans, and maybe even pay for some of your conference costs?

Learn as much as you can about the event. Websites usually include details regarding registering to be part of the book fair. You may have to contact the conference organizers to find out other information such as:

- Do you need to bring your own table coverings?

- How many copies of your books should you bring?

- How many people attended the previous book fairs held by this conference group and what do they expect this year's traffic to be like?

- What hours will the book fair be held?

- How many other book vendors will be in attendance?

- Is this fair genre specific or open to any kind of books?

- How will book sales be conducted, i.e. will you have to collect payment yourself or will it be handled through a central cashier?

- Does the conference require a royalty or a cut of your sales?

- Are you expected to decorate your own table?

- What about table signage? Does the show supply that or is it your responsibility?

- What are the taxes you'll be required to pay on your book sales and how is that handled if you're from out of province/state or country?

Once you have answers to these and other questions that might arise, you can prepare to get your books to the venue. However, before we go into that topic, you must first investigate the law regarding where you will be selling. For example, if you are from a different country from where the book fair is held, are you even allowed to import books, or other collateral products, and sell them at the fair?

Are there laws in place that allow you to import books but that don't allow you to do the selling yourself? Immigration laws sometimes prohibit a direct exchange of product for money as this can be deemed as working illegally. If that is the case, be sure to check with the conference to see what other arrangements can be made to facilitate your book sales.

Can you, for example, share a booth or table with a local or citizen of the country and allow him or her to sell your books? Will the book fair organizers sell your books for you?

All these questions are important considerations when planning to attend a book fair. Once you have satisfied all the conference and legal requirements, you can look forward to a pleasant experience meeting readers and selling your books.

Recording Your Efforts for Ultimate Success

As a writer, you may be wondering why would you want to record all of your efforts, even the failures?

I know from experience that I have repeated errors without realizing I had done this before and it did not work. So, why would I want to do the same thing all over again?

It comes down to memory. We all forget at a rapid rate whether we want to admit it or not.

Do you remember what you ate for lunch eight days ago or eighty-eight days ago? Not likely. The same holds true when marketing your books. You will certainly remember the successes and *some* of the failures but you will not remember the details. How can you stop repeating marketing blunders?

The answer is quite simple and here are some tips to help you along:

1. Record all of your marketing efforts in detail. I read many books and Dan Poynter, of The Self-

Publishing Manual fame, explains that you need to keep a record of all that you do when it comes to your book. He tells us that it is not just your marketing efforts that need to be recorded, you need to keep copies of all the press releases, the results from each, the coverage you get, the shares for quotes, and so on.

2. Work electronically as much as possible. I use OneNote and EverNote to keep track of my progress and the results. If I send out a press release, I have a tab for "Press Releases" with a master table to track where I send it and the response, then I add a page for each release with the wording and any other notes on feedback.

3. If you are technology challenged, use a binder and divide it into sections. Keep printed copies of all your correspondence and add a notes page for the details. Always add a front page in table format to track what you have done.

4. Never rely on your memory. There are too many balls up in the air to remember the exact details of what worked and what did not. Track, track, track until you are sick of it. You will never regret the ability to go back to get details.

5. Relax. Make tracking a natural part of what you do as you are in the process. If you are doing a press release, add it to your tracking system when you have finished writing it. This way you will

not add to the piles of work that you have to do "later".

Learning to track your marketing efforts as you do them will certainly help with your future marketing. You can go back and see where you sent your press releases and locate the ones where someone acted on the information. This way you can avoid sending your releases to publications that had no interest, thus saving time and effort.

It can be tempting to blast your press releases everywhere again but I recommend that you leave out the ones that did not respond until the end of your marketing campaign. Don't waste your precious marketing efforts on dead ends. By tracking everything, all the time, you will soon see patterns. Patterns provide you with a tool to better hone in on your target audience.

Basic Black and White, Colors Say it All

When it comes to branding, colors play an important role in your total image. Each color provokes a feeling or an emotion. What emotions are you trying to elicit when it comes to your book, book series, or personal brand?

In this article, we will walk you through the colors and how they affect readers.

Color response is generally broken down into three categories:

- Emotional response. The feeling a color gives you when you see it. Think about red—the emotional response is generally associated with anger or love, whereas blue makes us think peaceful and cool.

- Physical response. What would green indicate? Likely it would be focus or concentration while yellow would be bright or reflective.

- Behavioural response. Think of orange and it reminds us of fast food and movement while purple could be surprise or something royal.

46

Think of colors in terms of what you want as a reaction to your branding. There are many color variations for eliciting the response you want. The following is a list of various colors and what they represent.

- Blue: Tranquility, Security, Integrity, Peace, Loyalty, Trust, Intelligence, Cleanliness, Order, Sky, Water, Cold, Calm

- Turquoise: Spiritual, Healing, Protection, Sophistication, Calm, Water

- Green: Freshness, Environment, New, Money, Fertility, Healing, Earth, Nature, Youth, Jealousy, Inexperience, Envy, Misfortune, Vigor

- Yellow: Bright, Sunny, Energetic, Warm, Happy, Perky, Joy, Intellect, Summer, Gold, Philosophy, Dishonesty, Cowardice, Jealousy, Covertness, Deceit, Illness, Hazard, Betrayal, Optimism, Idealism.

- Purple: Royalty, Nobility, Spirituality, Luxury, Ambition, Wealth, Ceremony, Mysterious, Transformation, Enlightenment, Cruelty, Arrogance, Mourning.

- Pink: Healthy, Happy, Feminine, Sweet, Compassion, Playful, Love, Romance, Excitement

- Red: Love, Passion, Energy, Power, Strength, Heat, Desire, Anger, Excitement, Speed, Aggression, Blood, Fire, Danger, War, Violence, Intensity.

- Orange: Courage, Confidence, Friendliness, Success, Enthusiasm, Warmth, Vibrant, Expansive, Flamboyant, Demanding of Attention, Energy.

- Brown: Earth, Stability, Hearth, Home, Outdoors, Reliability, Comfort, Endurance, Simplicity, Comfort, Longevity, Conservative.

- Tan: Unification, Quiet, Pleasantness, Calm, Simplicity, Dependable, Flexible, Conservative.

- Gold: Wealth, Wisdom, Prosperity, Value, Tradition.

- Silver: Sleek, Graceful, High Tech, Sleek

- White: Goodness, Purity, Innocent, Fresh, Easy, Clean, Isolation, Pristine, Empty.

- Black: Protection, Elegance, Evil, Dramatic, Formal, Mastery, Death, Mystery.

Now it is your turn to look at the colors you are currently using, Do they represent the emotion, physical, and behavioural responses you want for your brand?

Beyond Bullets

I have seen many presentations where the presenter just reads the slides. What advice would you give for going beyond just the bullet points?

When you are first starting out as a writer and are doing presentations, the temptation is to use the PowerPoint presentation as a crutch. You put the information on the slide and then as a matter of comfort, you read them to make sure you do not miss anything. Unfortunately, doing this will let everyone know that you are an unseasoned presenter.

Thank goodness there are simple tricks to get beyond just reading the slide deck. Try these ideas as a starting point.

1. Use the 5 by 7 rule. No more than five bullets on a slide with a maximum of seven words each. I know this one is not always that easy to follow and at Author's Success Guild we push the boundaries by using animations and images.

2. Use images with captions instead of bullet points. You can illustrate your ideas with the right

graphic and a good caption and often this will have a longer lasting impression on your audience.

3. Use short videos embedded into your presentation. Create a "trailer" like those done for movies, that emphasizes your point and then discuss what people saw through a series of questions. You certainly cannot read a video on the screen but you do have to be quiet while it plays.

4. Make your presentation interactive by posing a question and filling in the blanks right on the presentation as you are giving it. This is a little more advanced and we tell you how to do this in other lessons. It is actually very easy to do but it does take a little practice to execute during a live presentation.

5. Involve the audience through polls and surveys inside your presentation and then, depending on the results, alter your presentation automatically. If you have five questions and each question leads into a different presentation, be prepared to change your presentation on the fly to accommodate audience needs. Yes, you will need to have five branches to your presentation. They can be prepared as one presentation using appropriate linking strategies.

Now for the hard part. Preparing your slide deck is simple as long as you know what you want to say. The more difficult aspect is practice! Yes, practice and rehearsal will make the difference between a great presentation and simply reading the slides.

The best ways to practice entail the following:

1. Sit in front of your computer with the webcam turned on.

2. Put your presentation and your presentation notes on the screen or as an alternative, print out what you want to say.

3. Use a free service such as zoom.us to allow for recording.

4. Run through your presentation while recording in front of your webcam.

5. Play back your recording. Remember the first run through will be the one where you are constantly looking at your notes.

6. Continue the recording and playback process at least ten times until you are spending most of the time looking at the camera and only glancing at the slide deck on occasion to keep your place. When you are happy with what you see, then you are almost ready for the live event.

7. Find a few people to rehearse with each day. Look at your presentation as your part in a Broadway show! The actors do not go on stage and read their scripts, and neither should you.

8. Get out there and do the presentation!

Giving is Getting When it Comes to Networking

I read a book about networking and one of the tactics mentioned is to constantly give and share. Other than sharing my book, what could I share?

As with any business book or non-fiction book, you may be a little hesitant to share what's inside. The fear is that people will keep asking for shared items until you have shared all of your secrets and everything that is in the book. I completely understand your hesitation. Let's take a look at what sharing can be like and how you can take advantage of the tactic.

Think about the research you did when writing your book. I am sure you did not use all the facts, figures, and insights that you picked up in your book. These snippets of research that go beyond your book are ideal for adding to your list of items you can share. This does not mean you have to memorize all of the information but you can assemble it in a list.

Before we get into tactics, what does sharing really mean?

When it comes to sharing while networking, you are likely thinking of sharing your knowledge. Knowledge is only one piece of the pie. You can also share written material, experiences, connections, clients, and even your time.

For example, when another person is having difficulty with an issue and you have experience in resolving the problem, you can readily share your story to help them. In turn that person will be very thankful and may think of you when it comes to using your expertise for a job.

Now what about the list we mentioned? Here are some easy sharing ideas you can implement right away.

1. Prepare a series of blog articles based on the research you conducted. That is, the material you did not put in the book but is still relevant to your expertise.

2. Create a mini video series using the same blog topics. The videos should be two to five minutes in length.

3. Open your client contact file and match up clients with members of your networking group. This list will be gold when it comes to offering introductions as needed.

4. Prepare a talk on your subject.

5. Create a list of questions from the conversations you have with members of your group. Prepare the answers ahead of time and offer this as a free report.

6. Always share what you know to help others and direct them to buy your book if they want to know more than what you are willing to share for free.

Sharing is easy. The more you share, the more people will want to share with you.

The World At Your Finger Tips Through Social Media

Social media has taken over as a method for getting noticed. How can you limit who sees you or is that a dumb idea?

If you are marketing you books, why would you want to limit who sees you unless you are thinking about your personal profile rather than your public figure profile.

Facebook makes it easy to have privacy settings on your personal page. You can limit what the world sees and what you share. Even with privacy settings, your friends could share your information without you knowing about it. Although this may work in the short term, just remember that whatever you post stays almost forever, so post only items that build your reputation and don't damage it.

Using pseudonyms for social media profiles for private postings is probably a better way to go. Keep your private life separate from your business life. Not everyone will share your interests and some will even take the time to pull you down for an interest they really dislike.

The decision is ultimately yours, though. Do you want to market your books or do you want to hide from the world?

Hiding is easy. Simply stay away from social media unless you are using it to keep track of friends. Do not accept friend requests and do not allow anyone to follow you. End of story. No one will ever learn about your book this way.

On the other hand, using social media in an intelligent way will give you the visibility you need without going overboard with the connections. It is a matter of balance.

Here are some ideas you may want to consider:

1. Create a profile for Facebook that you will use for promoting your book. This should be a separate profile from your personal one. This way you can keep your private life out of the public view.

2. Using that profile, set up a fan page for your readers.

3. Create a profile on Twitter, Pinterest, YouTube, Google+ using the same profile information as the one you set up for Facebook. This will create the Public Identity for you.

4. Create a Facebook group for insiders only - this is for your readers and it should also be based on your public profile.

5. Create a series of blog articles and an author resource box that links back to your new public profile. Use these articles to post in locations such as ezinearticles.com, americanChronicle.com, or BestEzineArticles.com.

When keeping your personal information private, you will absolutely need to create a new public profile to market your books. Make sure you post your personal items on your personal profile, and your book marketing items on your public profile. As long as you can keep it straight, you have the ability to limit who sees you.

Using Your Target as a List Building Weapon

Building email lists is far more difficult than I imagined. IS there a simple way to build the list targeting my perfect reader?

I hear it all the time—build your list and then make your sales. Sounds easy but when you ask how to do that, no one seems to know the right answer! We all know that the list is the most important piece of the sales process. A salesperson in any company relies on his connections to get the sale. And she also has to build new relationships at the same time.

The same is true for you as a marketer of your books. You need to build relationships with readers and then add them to your list. By building relationships, your readers will be more than willing to be a part of your list. Readers, generally, will not just jump on your list, they want to get to know you first, see if what you are offering fits their needs, and understand the benefits for them when it comes to being a part of your group.

What is comes down to is building your list with people who are interested in your genre, not just readers, but focused readers. This does not mean you build your list slowly by connecting with readers one at a time, it means building your list by being laser focused on your target.

Let's talk about Matt. Matt is an author of mystery novels and his focus is on a particular reader who loves looking for clues that are woven into the story. Matt knows that these readers collect books, read books from three other authors in the same genre, and they buy everything these authors write. He also knows where they interact and hang out on social media. Matt still has more to learn about these readers but he has a good starting place to start a relationship with the groups.

Matt finds four social media groups—two on Facebook, one on LinkedIn, and one on YouTube.

The goal for Matt is to join in the conversation using the profile he has for his public profile (the profile that his readers will see). He sets another goal to put up his webpage with a form to get on his mailing list and also has a bonus offer in order to entice readers to join his list. A final goal is to have a Facebook Fan page, a twitter profile, and a YouTube channel and to populate each with some initial content.

Matt is now ready to start interacting with the groups he located. Although this has been a bit of work in getting everything set up, Matt is now conversing with group members on a regular basis. It is through this interaction and people wanting to know more about him that his list is starting to grow. The more he shares his knowledge and makes comments, the faster his list grows.

Matt is not just joining social media groups, he is also building his own group at the same time. He is using his group to post great information and ask for opinions.

You will notice that Matt has never asked for the sale and never asked people to join his list. He is spending time with his readers and they in turn want to know more.

There are many more ways to build your email list, however, this is a great starting point. Readers like having a relationship with authors and you can build a great income from just that fact.

Advantages of Benefit Writing

I write a lot of articles each month and I am having difficulty thinking about reader benefits. Any ideas on ways to generate reasons for a reader to read my writing?

Believe it or not, readers do not care about you or your book, they only care about themselves and how your book will make them feel. So why do most authors talk about themselves and why readers should take the time to pick up their book and read it?

The usual answer is that you have to show you are the expert for your genre, and that enthusiasts are reading your books. And you can prove it with all of the reviews you have and the testimonials as well. Good for you, bad for getting your sales over the top.

Readers only want to know what is in it for them (WIIIFM). So why are you not simply telling your readers your name and then dive right into the benefits for the reader? Likely it is because you have been reading a lot of marketing hype that tells you to boast about your success. Not only your success but how others (the third party testimonial) feel about you and your writing.

Guess what, none of that really matters.

So what does matter when it comes to pushing your book and getting readers?

The short answer is Reader Benefits!

At Author's Success Guild, we spend a lot of time figuring out what the reader wants, not what we want when it comes to marketing our books, products, and services. As an author, you need to do the same.

If you are a non-fiction writer, the benefits are usually easy to figure out. You can do the following:

1. Take the table of contents and look at your chapter titles. Do they create excitement? If not, change the names to create that emotion and desire to read your book.

2. Have you stated the problem you want to solve in terms of the reader? Is the problem real and is there pain associated with your topic? If so, tell an emotional story to hook in your reader.

3. Do your problem solutions move readers to action? Are the solutions easy to implement? Can you develop a sense of relief through your book description?

4. Do you have a three-minute book trailer that drags the potential reader through the mud and resolves the pain?

If you write fiction - the road to reader benefits is a little more challenging.

1. Does your book summary grab the reader by the throat having them beg to find out more?

2. When viewing your book trailer, do you create a sense of anticipation so that the potential reader jumps into action and buys your book?

3. Are you providing chapter summaries on your website that draw your reader into your world?

4. What other bonuses and items are you providing when the reader buys your book?

Although there are many other ways you can use reader benefits, these are the ones we find work wonders.

Are you ready to promote reader benefits for your book?

Enhancing Your Podcast with Lists

I have a podcast that I do each month and I want to promote the new broadcasts as well as the previous episodes. Is it good etiquette to send an email to my current subscribers reminding them to share?

There are many ways to promote your podcasts. If you already have a list, then send out the latest link with an email that explains what is in it for the listener. I know we sound like a broken podcast when it comes to reader benefits, but this is the single most important aspect of marketing your book and recording.

Here are some suggestions for promoting your podcasts both present and past. You can also promote upcoming episodes at the same time. As a reminder, you do not want to send too many emails and you also do not want to crowd too many items into your communications.

1. Prepare an email template you will use for all your podcast announcements. At Author's Success Guild we have seen everything from the

narrow text format to over-kill on the information sent.

- Use a newsletter style format. This way you can add links to past recordings and prepare the audience for audios that are planned in the future.

- Make the emphasis on the current release. Use images, white space, and an emotionally appealing title and sub-title. Include a summary that emphasizes the benefits of listening to this episode.

- When providing a link to the recording, make it a button that is easy to see. So many podcasters leave this piece out and you often have to hunt for the right link to get to the podcast. You need to think in terms of one-click and you are done.

- On the side bar (preferably the right), create a section called Archives. Here you can list previous recordings. We suggest that you limit this to seven with a MORE... button for the complete list.

- Below the Archives section, include a section called NEXT UP. Add a title, the topic and an emotional tie in short summary. You can do this with an image to really catch the eye.

- Add social sharing buttons to make the email easy to share!

- Last but not least, always include a way for a reader to subscribe to your list.

2. Have all your social media profiles ready to allow sharing. Post your newest release on all your social media sites.

3. Post your latest release in groups that allow you to post.

4. Prepare a clickable image with a link back to the podcast to share on Pinterest, Twitter, and Facebook.

5. Prepare an article or two to add to LinkedIn, eZineArticles, and other article marketing sites. This article needs to promote the content of your podcast. You will need to post the link to the podcast in the author resource box. Look at the bottom of this post for how to put together an author resource box with links.

Asking readers to share is easy if you provide the means to do so easily. No one will go out of their way to share if your content does not resonate with them. Images and easy social sharing icons provide a one-click solution.

How to Capitalize on Your Writing Career with Press Releases

I want to do press releases for my new book's launch but I haven't any idea how to write an effective one. Can anyone help me with quick tips to make this happen so I don't tear my hair out?

Writing effective press releases is truly a skill! Not a lot of people do it right. Press releases are a dime a dozen, so to speak, and unless they stand out from the crowd, they are not likely to get noticed.

There are a few rules that need to be adhered to in order to use the proper format. These are not difficult. The biggest difficulty is getting your press release read and getting the right people to read it.

So let's look at what you can do to make this process very simple.

First, let's look at the formatting rules.

1. One-inch margins. White space makes it easier to read your release.

2. Double spacing is the maximum but you can use 1.5 spacing. Once again this makes your release easy to read.

3. Make it short (one page is best). Although you can use two pages, the likelihood of the second page being read is negligible.

4. Do not use abbreviations.

5. Proof read everything. If you have a grammatical error or spelling error, that fact will take over what you write and the delete key will be used quickly.

6. Use a catchy title and subtitle (the first five words are the key to catching attention.)

7. Include contact information. Why send a release if you are not giving the reader the ability to connect with you for more information. Include phone, email, and other ways to contact you plus include the best times to be reached.

8. Include pricing and availability of your book. Even if you book is only on Amazon, include that fact with the link to the book.

9. Use a quote out of your book. Find a quote that ties in with the release. Do not be random with your choice of quote. It needs to be poignant and relevant.

10. Prepare a media list for your release (be specific about who will get the release, not everyone wants to read it). Choose only connections that do book reviews!

Now, here are some simply ways to getting your press release read:

1. The goal of the first sentence is to have the second sentence read. It is that simple. If the person cannot get past your first sentence, then the rest of the release is not worth anything. Make you first sentence about the reader and how you can emotionally tie them into reading more.

2. The goal of the second sentence is to get them to read the third sentence. State your reader benefits, one sentence at a time, drawing in your reader. A press release is nothing more than another story with a twist. The twist is to create enough emotion to push the reader to read the next sentence.

3. Continue to do the same for the first paragraph. Writing five sentences in the opening paragraph with the goal of getting the reader to read the next sentence is crucial, however, the last sentence in the paragraph must drive the reader to read the next paragraph.

4. Add the details of your press release by infiltrating facts one emotion at a time. If you

can't grab the reader, then your press release will be subject to the delete button.

How to Minimize Your Advertising Expense Using Facebook Ads

I'm interested in doing some inexpensive advertising and I have heard that Facebook is the best way to go. Any tips on getting the most bang for my buck with Facebook ads?

Facebook ads seem very simple at first glance, but once you go a little deeper, you will discover that there are many ways to use your advertising. Controlling your costs should be at the top of your list before you begin. Costs can become huge if you do not take the time to figure out a budget for your advertising efforts.

Before you begin, here are some items you should consider when developing your ad:

1. Make your ad is relevant to your audience. Do not spray and pray with your demographic choices. Know your audience and their interests right down to the demographics. Targeting your audience will make the difference between a

successful ad and an ad that does not get you results.

2. Highlight benefits for your offering. Include your business name and key facts.

3. Use a call to action. People may read your ad and not do anything, especially if there is nothing to click on to get more information or Like your page. Be strategic in what you are offering as a benefit to those who follow through on the action you place in the ad.

4. Choose an image that relates to your offering. The image needs to have strong emotional appeal plus it should be clear, eye-catching, and visible even when reduced to a small size.

5. Create a landing page that presents what you promised in the ad. The page needs to be easy to understand, and easy for the visitor to get what they are looking for, even if it is simply joining your email list.

6. Customize your headline for maximum impact. Do not keep the default headline offered by Facebook. Create a series of headlines you would like to use. Attention-getting headlines also need to be relevant to your offering.

7. Prepare more than one ad. Create a series of ads with minor changes between them. This way you can track what works and what does not. Refresh

your ad content every few days so the ad does not get stale.

Once you have prepared several ads, you are ready to decide the best way to take advantage of the advertising offerings you can use with Facebook.

Here are some of the avenues you can use:

- Use advanced targeting options.

- Facebook Offers.

- Sponsored-Stories.

- Host a contest.

- Boost a post.

- Get your Facebook ads into the News Feed.

- Use "Like" ads.

- Hide valuable content behind a Like barrier.

- Use large photos and shortened links for blog posts.

- Use animated graphics for ads.

- Share your success story and get an Ads coupon.

How to Create an Artist's Platform Through Book Extras

I love being a writer and now I realize you can also create an artist platform just by using my illustrations and quotes. Is it wise to do so?

Welcome to the new world. Many publishers want to know your platform and they also want to know that you have an established audience for your books. You may be thinking, what is a platform and how can I develop my own without too much effort? After all, I am a writer, not a marketer.

First, let's talk about what a platform is and how you can start to build your own.

Your platform is how you will be connecting to your readers, present and future. You could connect with them using many tools. Your tools could include (and not be limited to) a website, a blog, Facebook, Twitter, Pinterest, YouTube, podcasts, and personal appearances. Although this seems like a list of many platforms, each tactic is a small part of your overall platform. Theoretically, a platform is a unique business model that sets you apart from your competition. This really means you work on a multi-dimensional model connecting various types of media for consumption by your readers.

Lots of words, but what can you do to create your own platform?

Since a platform can start anywhere, your goal is to connect with your readers. If you do not use online technology, then your platform could simply be conducting presentations. It is the place where you build authority, trust, and give attention to your readers.

Where to begin?

1. Build an online presence. This does not mean gruelling days of writing blog articles, posting to Facebook, Twitter, developing quotes in graphic form, writing articles to share, and participating in a group or two. You can build your presence by adding value on a regular basis. There is no need to go overboard! Set up a schedule and adhere to it as you would any other routine. Your presence will grow.

2. Show your attitude at all times. Are you someone readers can relate to or are you someone they would not like on a personal level? The choice is yours and all of your online efforts, including

your personal entries are visible whether you like it or not.

3. Create more books and book related products as part of your platform. Most people do not make a living writing books but they do make a living from adding other products to the mix. If you write fantasy, your other products could include jewelry from the story, character development techniques, memberships into your world, and fan fiction entries. The list is actually quite long and only your imagination is a deterrent. Sell screensavers with your illustrations, sell a book of illustrated quotes; sell the images on their own. All of these will bring in more income and build your online presence at the same time.

Publishers will often look on the web to see if you are a person with whom they want to work. If you do a great job of being present, positive, and progressive, then you are likely to be a person of interest. If you are planning on going the self-publishing route, then your platform becomes even more significant.

Either way, build that platform and be a contributor and a producer of additional products that are related to your book. The more people get to know you, the more they will trust you, and the more they will buy from you.

The Perfect Reader

I have a pretty good idea of my perfect reader but I'm not sure how to find them or reach them. How can I connect with these people who would want my book, if they only knew about it?

Having a pretty good idea and knowing for sure will make the difference between getting the right connections and wasting time marketing to your list. But how do you make sure you know your who your perfect reader really is?

This is where you will need to put in some time and effort to build the foundation upon which you can market with pinpoint accuracy. Amazon keeps track of you and they know what you have been looking for, so their ads and suggestions are all based on what you have researched. I find this really interesting as when I was looking for the ideal drawing table for my office, I looked at quite a few models and finally came up with one I liked. Over the next week or so, the ads for the exact table kept appearing whenever I was in my browser doing my regular work. And when I went to Amazon, low and behold, an ad for the table appeared. Talk about targeting me for my interest! I also noticed the same is true when I buy books in a certain genre, the offers for other books and what others have read start appearing! My preferences are known and to them I am the perfect reader for similar books.

This type of information is exactly what you need to know to find your perfect reader!

In theory, this seems very easy, but in reality it does take a great deal of time and effort. However, once you have achieved success with your definition, getting to that reader is much simpler.

Here are some ideas and suggestions for finding your perfect reader:

1. Find a writer who writes in the exact genre as you and ranks in sales numbers on Amazon. This means right down to the sub-category. Don't waste your time on books that are not high on the sales list.

2. Make note of all the details. Use OneNote or EverNote to keep track of the information.

3. Look at the bottom of the description to find what others bought in that same genre. Make note of this information as well.

4. Take the author information for each notation and do a web search to locate their webpage, social media profiles, and any groups in which they participate. Add this information to your notation.

Spend the time you need to get the information. I suggest you find a minimum of five authors to start.

Now, let's look at ways you can connect with the readers of your genre.

1. If you have not already done so, create your own social media profiles and post to them on a regular basis.

2. Prepare an author resource box that you will use for each posting. See mine below for an example. Here I am promoting Authors Success Guild and looking for people to join my LinkedIn Group. You could drive people to your website or other location.

3. Join the groups you discovered while doing your research. These groups, depending on their size, and reader activity will provide you with insights into your perfect reader and what they are looking for.

4. Start adding to the discussions so that readers will get to know you. Readers will buy from those

that they feel they know and trust. Be that person!

There are many more ways you can connect with your ideal reader to increase your sales. The most important thing to remember: Be approachable, let the readers get to know you, and they will follow.

Dr. Bette Daoust is a best-selling author, speaker and consultant to small business. She works with authors and speakers to support them in their marketing efforts. Bette is a part of the founding group at http://AuthorsSuccessGuild.com and is the CEO of Vervial Group Consulting International, Inc. Follow her on Twitter @DrBette or join her group on LinkedIn:

http://LinkedIn.com/groups/Authors-Success-Guild

Wendy Dewar Hughes is an author and a book coach, and provides publishing assistance to independently published authors through her company, Summer Bay Press. She is also a professional artist and book cover designer. Wendy is a founder at Author's Success Guild and owns several websites providing products and services for writers and artist. Follow her on Twitter @WDewarHughes, and on Facebook and Pinterest at Wendy Dewar Hughes - Author. She can also be found at:

http://AuthorsSuccessGuild.com

www.ingramcontent.com/pod-product-compliance
Lightning Source LLC
Chambersburg PA
CBHW050554280326
41933CB00011B/1837